Loveship

poems by

Ed Gold

Finishing Line Press
Georgetown, Kentucky

Loveship

ACKNOWLEDGMENTS

I am grateful to the publishers of the following poems:

Ark, *Kakalak*
Eye to Eye, *Rat's Ass Review*
Loveship, *Passager*
Prayer of the Cicada, *Rising Phoenix Press*
Puzzle, *Cyclamens and Swords*
Spring Molt, *Shakespeare and Friends*
Texas Hold 'em, *Masters Poker League Poker Poems* (UK)
The Next People, *The Ekphrastic Review*
Valentine, *New York Quarterly*
Waiting for Amy in Front of the TV, *Kansas Quarterly*
Woke up this morning, *Star 82*
ZXCVBNM, *Window Cat Press*

I am particularly grateful to Richard Garcia and the Long Table poets for
their support and friendship.

Publisher: Leah Huete de Maines
Editor: Christen Kincaid
Cover Art: *Reassembled Heart* by Meryl Weber
Author Photo: Amy Robinson
Cover Design: Elizabeth Maines McCleavy

Order online: www.finishinglinepress.com
also available on amazon.com

Author inquiries and mail orders:
Finishing Line Press
PO Box 1626
Georgetown, Kentucky 40324
USA

Contents

For everyone I have loved, still love,
and will love

WAITING FOR AMY IN FRONT OF THE TV

You are cashmere bouquet,
oil of olay,
dove, joy.

I am bird's eye, deep blue,
wheat and rice and corn chex
over you.

I wish we had nine lives
of suds and spin and tumble dry
in a gentle heat,

my pears, my sunkist,
my luckiest of all
lucky strikes.

VALENTINE

I am over 18 years of age
Yes I want to know how to
get girls through hypnotism

I have checked the box
next to the words

I have enclosed my
please rush me my

SIGNALS

blink twice
if you love me
but have been afraid to say

blink twice
if you are carrying
a concealed weapon

blink twice
if the red X of the sniper
has found us

blink twice
if doctors put tiny cameras
in your brain while you slept

blink twice
if the lord put the fossils in the ground
to test your faith

blink twice
if you are reading this poem
against your will

blink twice
if you want me
to rescue you

UNE FEMME COMIQUE

He was desperate to see the face
of every woman with blond hair
he saw from behind.
She would turn around and always be
the wrong one.
(The wrong one? Was he looking for someone?)

In a flash it came to him:
the woman of his mornings
since he first could read,
the woman whose image
smudged off the newsprint
all over him.
(He was in love with Winnie Winkle.)

He wrote her writer,
sent a resume, letters of recommendation from
his rabbi, his creative writing teacher,
the head of his department,
and he got the job—
the curly-haired English teacher
whom Winnie meets in school.

Ecstasy! Three frames a day
to be near her, to touch her
in the small public squares,
and the colors of Sunday!
It was all written: love, engagement.
Bonnaz buzzed with bridal designs.
Tu Tu and Birdie flew in from Pago Pago.

On the way to the wedding,
he was killed in a car-crash.
In the middle of a Meanwhile,
Winnie began her grief,
which lasted thirty-two frames.

TEXAS HOLD 'EM
for Ivy and David Berney

The hardest thing
is to get away from
a gorgeous loser,

but after the flop,
if you don't hit,
you gotta drop.

Say goodnight
to that pocket pair,
that ace-king suited.

Don't kid yourself:
you have nothing.
Get out before it gets expensive.

You flash me
the pretty cards
you dropped with.

What do you want me to say:
that you aren't so stupid
after all?

I know: you had it won at the turn
and lost it on the river.
wah wah wah.

Listen, until you see the river,
you don't even know
what you have.

I know how you feel.
I've released so many dazzling losers
into the muck.

TOUCH ME NOT

All day long,
you were my honey cups:
your fragrance weakened me;
my smooth meadow beauty,
curling eight anthers toward me;
my little floating heart,
white bells on slender,
filiform stems.

All night,
you were my shadow witch,
pale orchid from the West Indies;
my blazing star,
delicious to moths;
my carolina moonseed,
named for the shape
of the stone in the shell.

So why this morning,
were you prickly ash,
numbing my lips;
southern sheep-kill
the goats avoid like poison;
why are you sour grass,
your male and female flowers
on their separate stalks?

How all afternoon
did I become
stinking fleabane;
bastard toadflax
(nothing but a parasite);
bitter gallberry,
my fruit oozing
such black ink?

THE FLOWERS LEFT OVER FROM THE LAST POEM

It was one of those days in the south:
the azaleas were clammy,
and the trout lilies were flashing their dimples.

While undoing Barbara's buttons,
I spotted the bachelor's breeches.
Fortunately, she had hidden the hatpins.

I ran out into the toothache grass
and found her sleeping in the sneezeweed,
having bad dreams under the fever tree.

The wind twisted
the southern obedient-plants,
and they held their shape.

Just then, the deceptive spinypod
confused the trillium, and here came
the winged monkey flowers.

We hid under the purple toadshade
and watched the frogs shoot their arrows
into the fire wheel.

Now we hunker down to wait
for the Carolina wicky
to arrive with the sacred bean.

May we be blessed with everlasting peas
and Allegheny live-forevers
in the common glory of morning.

ARK

I don't know what possessed us
to eat the doves.

We were so drunk,
and you were wearing that green dress.

It wasn't like we didn't have
a boatload of other choices:

two of everything that wasn't extinct
for god's sake, but no,

we had to have those delicious,
delicious doves.

Since then,
we have floated blind,

hoping we bump up against land
before we devour everything.

WOKE UP THIS MORNING

on the wrong side of the bed,
in the wrong bed,
wrong part of town.
wrong town.

May a helicopter
yank me up out of here
and drop me down
on the right side

of the right bed
by you.
Stay put:
I will find you.

If I get there and
you are out searching for me,
we will miss each other
again.

ANNOUNCEMENT

Jennifer Stevenson, Episcopalian,
of New York City,
(née Baltimore, née Jewish, née Wendy Gold)
announces with profound regret
the dissolution of the marriage
of her parents

Julius and Celeste

without ceremony
in their northwest Baltimore home
after thirty-five years.
The marriage is survived by
Ms. Stevenson and her brother Chuck,
née Charles.

The family is requested to take sides.

JAZZ FEST
for Margaret Coleman and Brandt Saunders

SWAMP CAT DESCRIBES OUR LANDLADY

"She wakes up, takes a shower,
and sticks her tongue
in an electric socket."

ON THE PORCH AT 6TH AND CONSTANCE

Frank, our new Brazilian friend, reveals
he is related to Anne Frank.
"But" he hastened to assure us,
"I'm not Jewish!"
Thank God for that, Frank!

A THUMB

I meet Mark.
He shows me his half-thumb,
caused by his misuse of a saw.

He stares into my soul
and asks, "Do you walk with God?"
I do, I say.

He shakes my hand and leaves.
I am glad to see him go so quietly.

SWAMP CAT AND DT, AFTER HOURS

He: "I think I am done."
She: "Buzzed with no lips at a quarter past two."

HEAVEN

Sitting on a blanket with my baby
under the tree at Fais Do Do,
eating a soft-shell crawfish poboy,
listening to zydeco.

PUZZLE

words from crossword puzzle,
Charleston Post and Courier

In the southeast quadrant,
I thought the answer was insults,
but insults turned out to be intuits,
joining Iowa with Wessex,
which meant the southeast corner was done,
leaving only the heart open.

Then the Neva ran through St. Petersburg,
Linear B was the ancient Minoan language
not yet deciphered,
and a bass sax led to x-ray eyes.

But when Linear B turned out be A,
I learned that the Latin word for lover
is amateur,
and that solved a very difficult puzzle.

PUNISHMENT

after The Very Old Man with Enormous Wings,
by Gabriel Garcia Marquez

I feel so bad for the girl who was struck by lightning and transformed into a giant spider just for disobeying her parents and sneaking away to a dance. I was there, too, that night. I held her in my arms more than once and twirled around with her. I watched her disappear into the dark forest on her way home.

I feel so sad for that cute face and curly black hair on the body of a tarantula, bigger than a goat, with eight hairy legs in a cage in a carnival where people pay to view her and ask her personal questions.

That's why I make meatballs every day and toss them into the circle of her open mouth. At first, I only used salt, pepper, and Worcestershire sauce, but then I added oregano and thyme. Currently, I am doing turkey balls.

I don't know what she prefers, but every time I approach, she opens her mouth into a sad O for me to toss them in so I guess she likes all of the variations, or tolerates them, or just accepts that this is what she has to eat to stay alive.

I don't know what she will eat when the carnival finally leaves. Maybe it came here to set up its tents and its rides and die in our town. Maybe she will stay with me. Maybe she will live in the garage, stroll through the big back yard, and eat the aphids off the tomato plants.

Why do I care? Because I began life as a tarantula. When I defied my mother, a lightning bolt turned me into what I am today—a miserable creature with only two legs to walk on and a brain that can never forget what I have lost. I dream of waking up into the world of my parents as if nothing ever happened, as if my disobedience and cruel punishment were just scenes in a nightmare, and I gallop off on my eight legs in perfect synchrony.

I shake the turkey meatballs on their baking pan and watch them roll. I added rosemary to this batch.

MAKING A LONG STORY SHORT

I barked up so many wrong trees,
counted so many chickens before they hatched,
bit off so much more than I could chew.

I pulled so many legs,
so much wool over so many eyes,
so many rugs out from under.

Which is why I was alone
at the end of my rope,
with all my bridges burning.

So I went back to square one,
put my ducks in a row,
and got the show on the road.

With all my eggs in one basket,
I let the cat out of the bag
and put you on the spot.

We saw eye to eye,
and we were tickled pink.
We tied the knot with bells on.

Now we're neck and neck
in the nick of time, and your name
is on the tip of my tongue.

THE NEXT PEOPLE
after Linda Fantuzzo, Mythic Realm

The last thing we did was paint the ceiling green.
We had put it off forever.
Then you walked out the door into the busy light,
and I climbed up the gleaming ladder
and closed the window.

Above the empty fireplace,
we left the painting of the rainforest
we bought in Costa Rica.
Neither of us could imagine
looking at it in another room.

We left the door open for the sun to paint
a door of dappled light on the shiny floor
for the next people who will fill
this hollow space,
hoping for a different ending.

SPRING MOLT

I love how your auriculars
just cover your ear holes.
I love the circles
around your eyes.

I love your nape,
your bend of wing,
the undertail coverts
on your rump.

I gape at you
in your new plumage—
your bright axillars,
contours, and powder down.

I will follow you
to any canopy or understory
and be your mate
and nest with you.

QUERY LETTER FOR CHRYS TOBEY

My imaginary love and I have been together
fifteen or sixteen years.
from Love Poem, by Chrys Tobey

Are you in the market for a new imaginary love?
Fifteen or sixteen years is long enough,
don't you think?

I'm getting closer to dumping mine.
Really pretty,
but too high maintenance.

I can provide references.
I have performed these imaginary services
many times over the years.

I promise never to discuss farting.
I promise to send you pictures
of any of my body parts you ask me to.

I will hide my Baltimore accent
and learn to talk
like a person from Hoboken.

I can pay off the balance of your student loans
that your current imaginary love
hasn't already paid.

We can go on imaginary dates
to some incredible places
and do unspeakable things.

You can write new poems
inspired by my quirks
and dedicate them to me.

I, too, have an armpit
in which you could cuddle up
and sleep like a dead person.

ZIGGY MEETS ZOE

Va-va-voom!
Ooh-la-la!
Hubba hubba!

"Psst..."
"Ahem..."
"Yoo hoo!"

"Huh?"
"Eh?"
"As if."

Oops.
Ouch.
Jeez.

"Hmm."
"Oh well."
"Why not?"

Lo and behold!
Holy guacamole!
Who knew?

ZXCVBNM

Zoe's xylophone comes via bonded, nervous messenger.
Zoe's xylophone can vibrate beyond normal music.

Ziggy exposes criminal violence by necrophilic matadors.
Ziggy examines cranial varieties—beans, noggins, melons.

Zoe's x-rated career veers between naked mountains.
Zoe's x-rayed child vanishes behind nightmares.

Ziggy explores crypts very boldly, never meekly.
Ziggy exhumes cardiac victims before new moon.

Zoe's ecstasy conjures visions besides neck massage.
Zoe expects casual violation but needs more.

Ziggy excites coyotes, vanishes before night melts.
Zoe exactly counts vanilla beans next morning.

Ziggy's exit cures viruses, but nerves matter.
Zoe exhausts chocolates, vainly battles nocturnal madness.

CROSSING

The oars ply me toward the forgetting
so I can be cleansed
and come back again blank.

I already forgot what time I am due,
what I am supposed to wear, and
whether I should have brought something.

Maybe you are going to be there?
I hope I recognize you.
Maybe if I could hear your voice

or smell your perfume,
I would remember whether
I want to remember you.

PRAYER OF THE CICADA

Both of my tymbals twitch
at exactly the same moment,
and my abdomen swells
with the resonance of the Lord,

Who kept me blind
in underground chambers
for so many years
to suckle at cypress roots,

Who ignited my eyes,
impelled me to tunnel up,
climb a tree, moult my shell,
and blossom,

Who bestowed unto me
these four translucent wings,
this black carapace propelling
through the bliss of space and light.

Oh Lord, let me remain among the uneaten
long enough to find my mate on a limb
and buzz together for a little while
in this dazzling emptiness.

THE WARNINGS THAT CAME WITH THE CHAIR

We did not ignore all the warnings:
we did not stand on the chair, and
we did not use it as a stepladder.

But I must admit we did not check the bolts
every three months and retighten them.
We don't even know where the bolts are.

We never examined the chair
for a missing, damaged, or worn part,
and we didn't stop using the chair

until the part was replaced
by a new part,
which only the manufacturer could supply.

And while I was sitting in the chair,
I asked you to sit on the armrest,
hoping you would say yes.

We were so lucky:
serious injury could have occurred
because it clearly states

that the chair is designed
for only one person,
and once you accepted my invitation

and sat down,
we soon were both on the chair
and in it,

exceeding the safety capacity
by a factor of two,
exposing us to a range of risks.

We were lucky to survive
our failure to heed
the printed warnings.

I LOVED YOU BEFORE I KNEW I LOVED YOU

I loved you before our first date
at the Folger Theater on Capitol Hill
to see the Tempest (you say)
or Henry IV, Part I (I say).
We agree it was dinner at the Hawk 'n' Dove,
but we don't remember what we ate.

I loved you before I saw you
in that green dress.
Why else did I give your boyfriend
such a hard time about how he treated you?
"What the hell do you care?" he asked me.
What the hell did I care?

A year before, I flew to Paris to visit
the girlfriend before you,
and in the middle of the first night
she emerged from the bathroom,
and I thought she was you.
I didn't know yet that I loved you.

That was almost a year before
our first date at the Folger
when the big bang created our new universe,
which could not be contained in the future,
which leaned back into the past
and warped the pillars of time forever.

CARE AND FEEDING

We love when they rebloom
in such preposterous purples,
or yellow laced with red veins,
or white like my grandfather's socks.
They are all different ages,
but now all six are blossoming.

It's because Amy found their sweet spot
by the sliding glass doors that face south,
and because once a week, on Thursdays,
I speak lovingly to them
as I place three ice cubes
around each green stalk.

Maybe that's what it takes to rebloom:
the right light, a slow drip, a little cooing.

CONFESSIONS OF NOAH'S DOVE

On my first flight, I found dry land.
I came back and lied:
I wasn't ready to disembark.
I needed to say goodbye,
but where were you?

On my second flight,
even the branches were dry,
but still I kept quiet.
That night, you let me find you.
When the sun came up,
I took off and didn't look back.

I claimed the perfect perch
in a green olive tree,
watched the ark blunder ashore,
the survivors kissing the sand,
thanking the Lord for deliverance.

I thanked God, too,
when you chose my nest
of twigs, grass, and pine needles
in which to settle your soft feathers.

FUGUE FOR THE FIRST GRANDCHILD

Amy and I are going to be grandparents.
Our daughter called to tell us.
It's their first: he will be an itchy ginger.
But we can't tell anyone yet.

The subject bobs up again:
Amy and I are going to be grandparents,
even as my mind tries to move on.
How can we not tell anyone?

What else is there to talk about?
Our chain is now connected to the future.
Amy and I are going to be grandparents:
we have handed over the magic beans.

Each time I almost get away from it,
the same thought floats up
like the answer in a magic 8-ball:
Amy and I are going to be grandparents.

Amy and I are going to be grandparents.
I hope you haven't heard:
that means someone we swore to secrecy
betrayed us like we did when we told them.

But if you think the idea that
Amy and I are going to be grandparents
is something we can take in quietly,
without giggling and blithering,

then I don't know what I can tell you.
Who thought we'd get this old together?
Amy and I are going to be grandparents,
and we are not taking this lightly.

We are happy to be here.
At our age, some of the best are long gone
along with some of the worst,
but Amy and I are going to be grandparents.

LOVESHIP

That eye-bite you flashed me,
was it an amoret or a blench?
Are you my half-marrow,
or are you just foading me?

I am mally of your fernticles and murfles.
I swingle in the crisples of your hair.
I linger at your heart-spoon,
the soft curve of your nuddle.

Let's shab out to the sky parlor
under the dream hole
and smick together and snoozle
and quaggle all over like jelly.

Don't be carked:
there will be no afterclap.
I am no mere belly-friend or franion,
no wowf performing murlimews.

We are side by side
in the kissing crust,
and it smells like
cloves and oranges.

Born in Baltimore, Ed is a graduate of the Johns Hopkins University Writing Seminars and taught for many years at the University of Maryland. He has two chapbooks, *Sundown and Owl,* and poems in the *Ekphrastic Review, Petigru Review, New Verse News, Think, New York Quarterly, Kakalak,* and many others. His poems have won awards from the South Carolina Poetry Society. Ed runs the Skylark poetry contest for SC high school poets and is a co-curator of the Sundown Poetry Series for Piccolo Spoleto. A grateful member of Richard Garcia's Long Table Poets, Ed lives in Mount Pleasant, South Carolina, with his wife Amy and their dog Edie.